I Saw We Saw

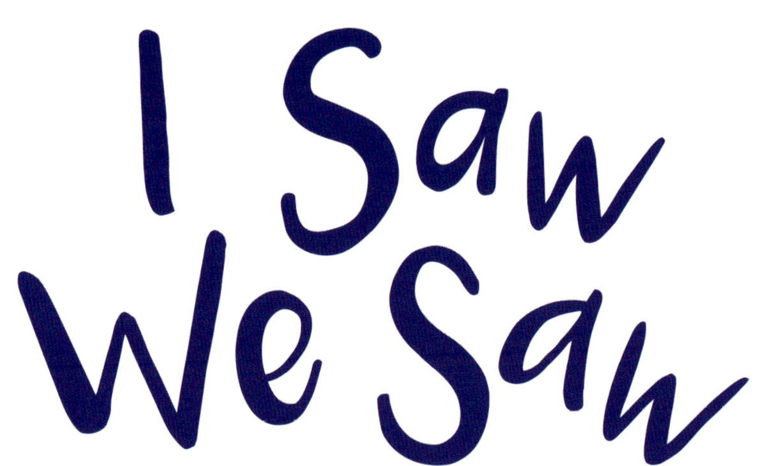

By Yolŋu students at Nhulunbuy Primary School
with Ann James & Ann Haddon

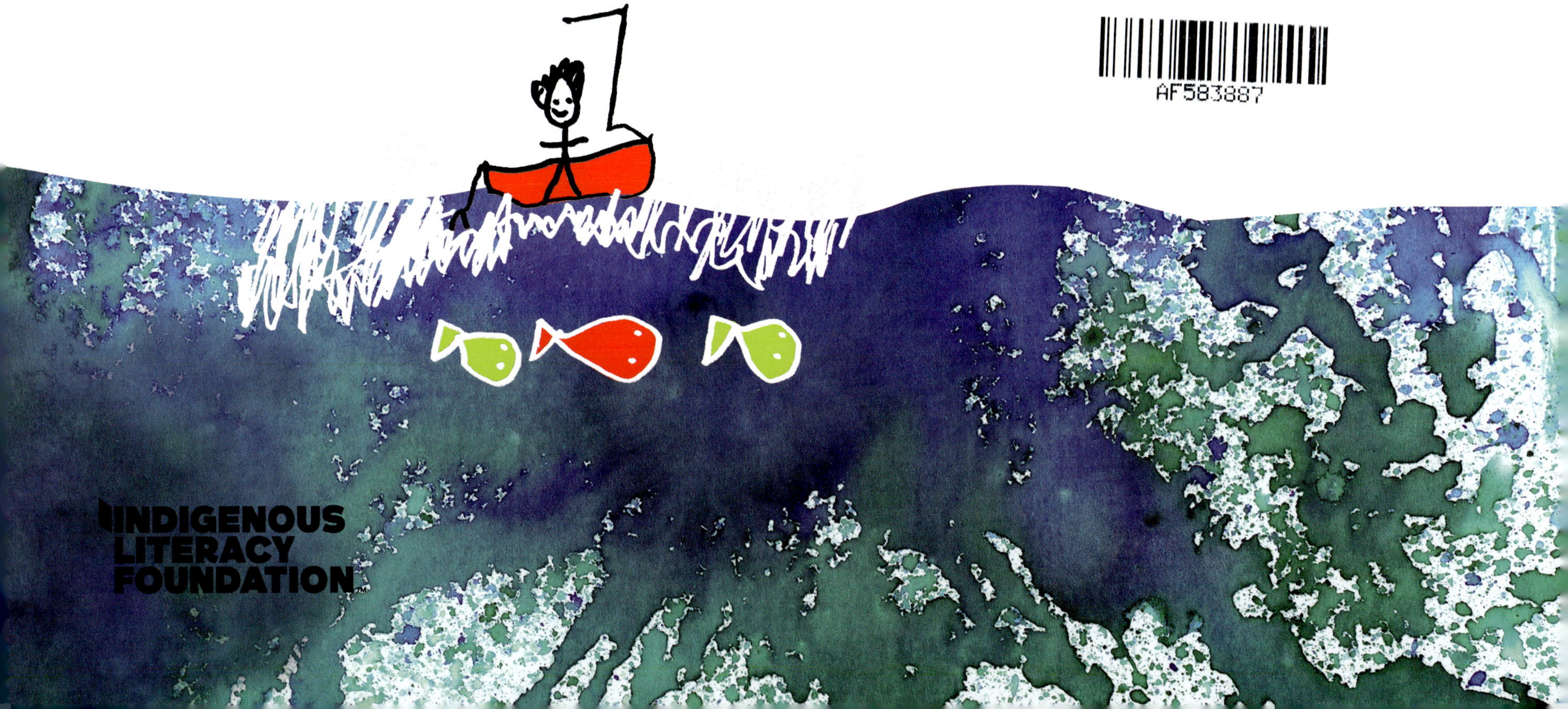

INDIGENOUS LITERACY FOUNDATION

About the Indigenous Literacy Foundation

The Indigenous Literacy Foundation (ILF) is a national charity working with Aboriginal and Torres Strait Islander remote Communities across Australia. We are Community-led, responding to requests from remote Communities for culturally relevant books, including early learning board books, resources, and programs to support Communities to create and publish their stories in languages of their choice.

In 2024 the ILF won the Astrid Lindgren Memorial Award, given annually to a person or organisation for their outstanding contribution to children's or young adult literature.

First published in 2019 by the Indigenous Literacy Foundation
This paperback edition published in 2025

Gadigal Country
Level 17/207 Kent Street
Sydney NSW 2000
ilf.org.au

Cataloguing-in-Publication details are available from the National Library of Australia

www.trove.nla.gov.au

ISBN 9781923456952

Typesetting and design by Lee Burgemeestre

Printed in China by RR Donnelley Asia Printing Solutions Limited

Yolŋu

Yolŋu are the Indigenous Australian people of north-east Arnhem Land in the Northern Territory of Australia. With country that ranges across 97,000 square kilometres, Yolŋu are considered one of the largest Indigenous groups in Australia. Yolŋu literally means 'person' in Yolŋu Matha, the main language spoken by the people. This language comprises twelve sublanguage groups, each with its own Yolŋu name. English is a second (or third or fourth) language for most Yolŋu children.

I Saw, We Saw is written in English with some words in the Dhanu sublanguage of Yolŋu Matha. The tailed 'ŋ' is pronounced 'ng' as in 'song'.

Hover your phone camera over the code to hear a reading of the book

There's lots to see in Yolŋu country.

I saw a **gurruṯuminy** playing on the sand.

We saw a **wa<u>t</u>u** grab a stick from a man.

I saw a **djeṯ** looking in the **gapu**.

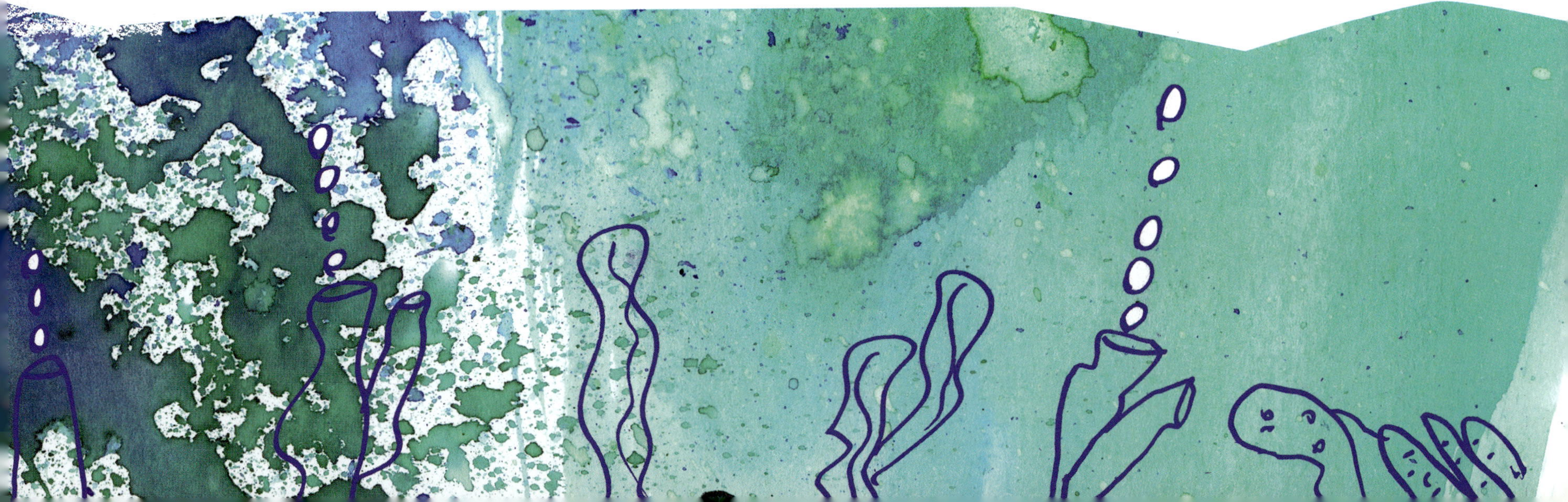

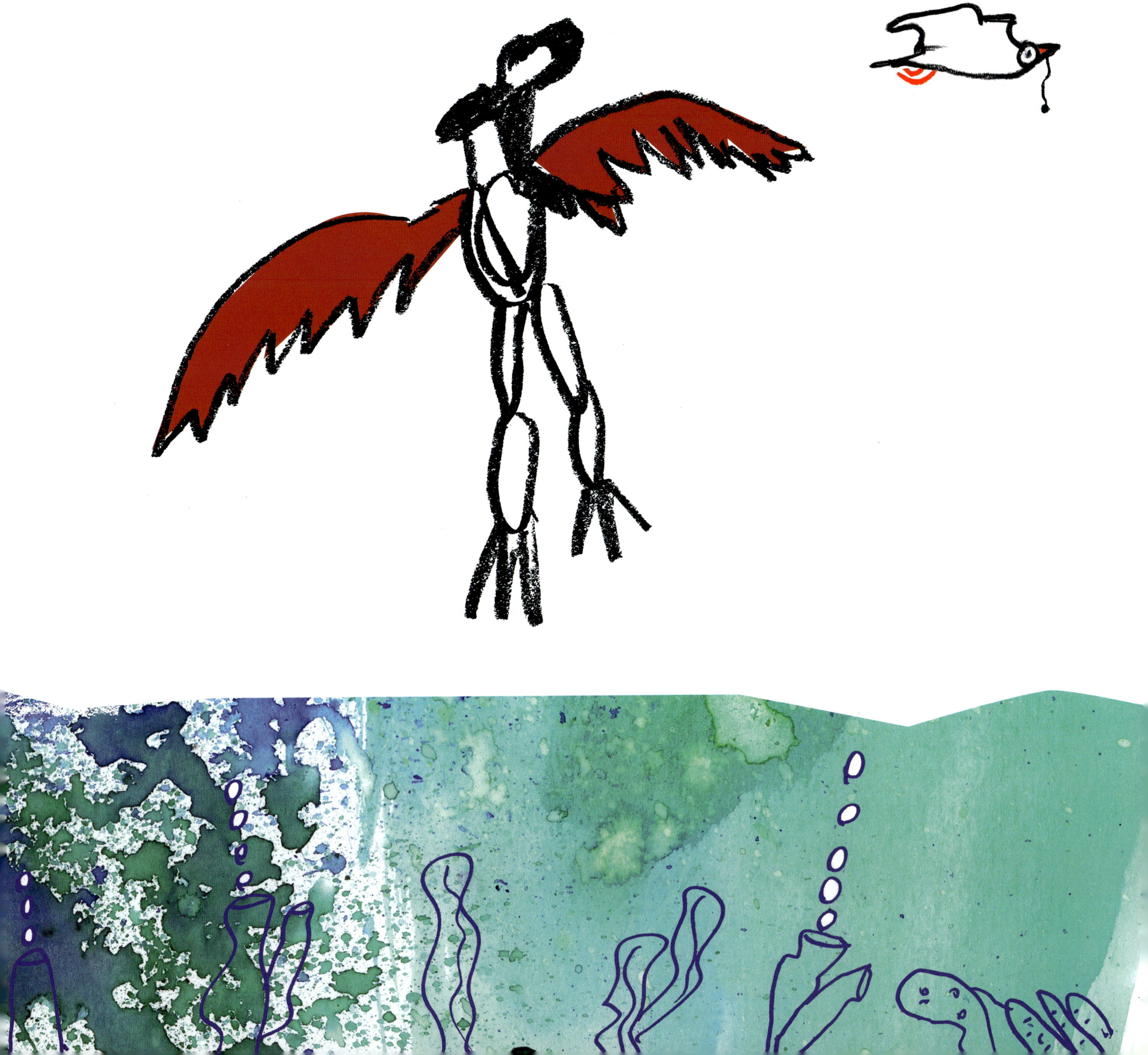

We saw kids collecting **mapu**.

I saw a **maranydjalk** leaping high.

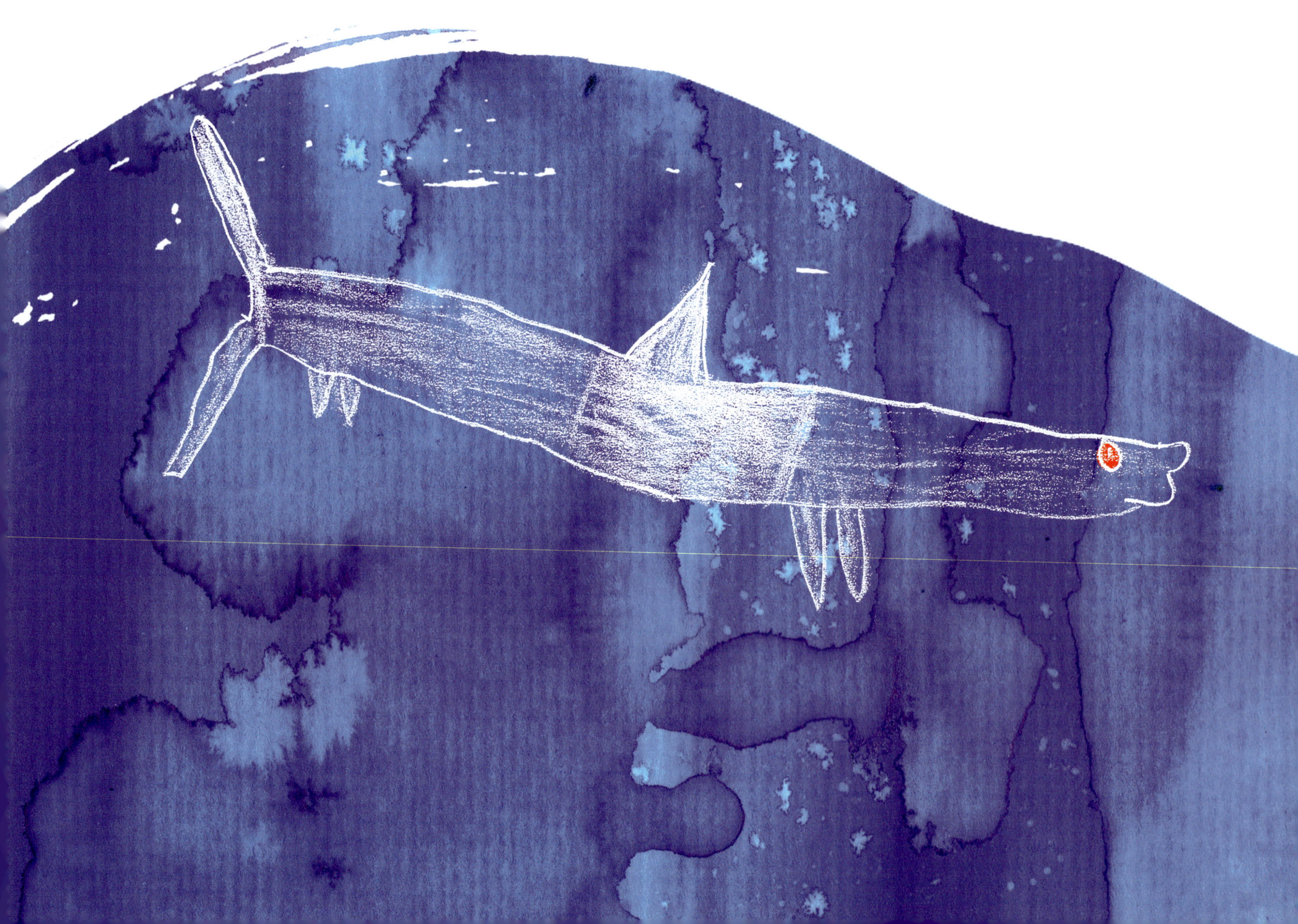

We saw a **ŋurula** soaring in the sky.

I saw a **bäru** big and scary.

We saw **wäkuṉ**, timid and wary.

I saw a **mirinyiŋu**. Look at his eye.

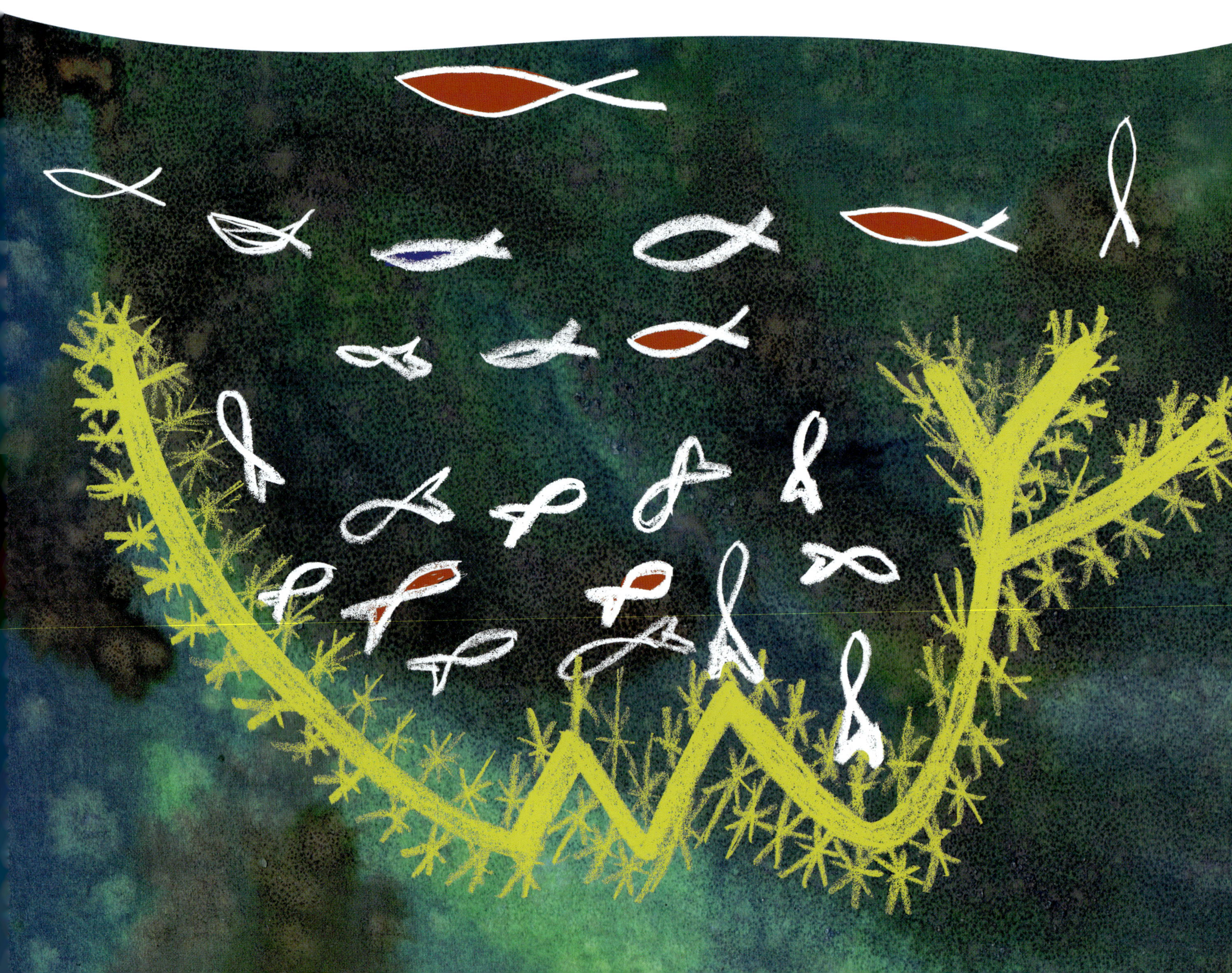

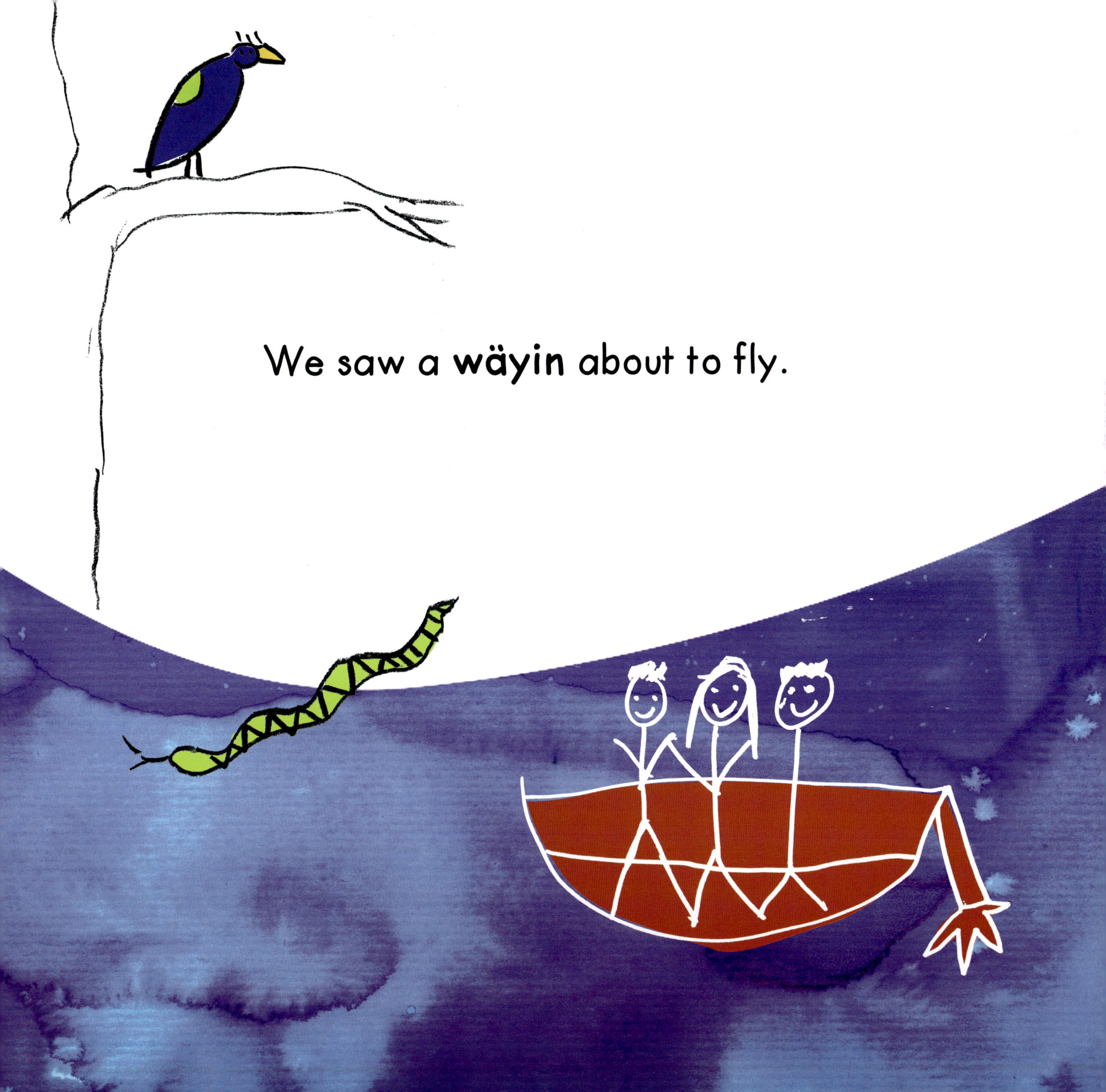

We saw a **wäyin** about to fly.

I saw the **walu** looking at me.

We saw **d̲epina** crawling on a tree.

I saw **mattjurr** flapping in the sky.

We saw **wärraŋ**. Feathers will fly.

I saw **ŋamaḻa** returning to the nest.

We saw our Yolŋu country,

it's the **best**!

What did you see?

Stingray
Seagull
Crocodile
Mullet/Little Fish
Whale
Bird/Kingfisher
Sun
Caterpillars
Bats
Chickens
Mumma
Family
Dog
Eagle
Water
Turtle Eggs

rock
Ski Beach
Town Lagoon
Ski Beach
Hospital
golf club
Boat Club
church
Lions Park
Skate_Park
BMX
Woolies
Town Oval
BP
Yirrla

Nhulunbug

Acknowledgements

The Indigenous Literacy Foundation would like to thank the Yolŋu students of the Nhulunbuy Primary School for their commitment to this project, and also the staff, in particular, Shane Ogg, whose assistance on this project was invaluable. We'd also like to thank Lisa Dhurrkay, and the Yirrkala School Literature Production Centre who provided additional language support.

And a big thank you to Ann James and Ann Haddon for inspiring and supporting the students as they created this book, and to Lee Burgemeestre for adding the magical designer's touch.